Somebody Say "Glory"

During the late 1940s and early 1950s, the lives of five ordinary men and five ordinary women were on a trajectory to do extraordinary things for God. Ed and Marilou McCully, Jim and Elizabeth (Betty) Elliot, Nate and Marj Saint, Roger and Barbara Youderian, Pete and Olive Fleming would become known the world over because of the deaths of the five Christian missionary men in the jungles of Ecuador in January 1956 at the hands of a savage people group known as the Aucas.

However, the words and deeds of these five couples prior to that fateful day, and the continued faithfulness the widows showed in the years thereafter, are what makes the story of their lives, and deaths, so remarkable.

While some literary license has been taken for the purpose of moving the story along, this play is the result of years of research, and every effort has been made to tell the story as truthfully as it was lived. The author read numerous books, magazine articles, and newspaper accounts related to the lives of these five families. She researched letters and journal entries made by the men, watched documentaries, and interviewed their fellow laborers on the mission field, Ralph and Marion Stuck. The author would like to make special acknowledgement of the invaluable insight and information provided by the Stucks.

The Play Script is an original copyrighted work by Martha Ford Fry and based on actual events. The play was original created to be a musical featuring the songs of Casting Crowns. However, the songs made famous by Casting Crowns are original works copyrighted by their respective authors. As a result, performance rights must be obtained from each copyright owner in order to perform any song not in the Public Domain with this play. Realizing that this may become a financial burden for small amateur groups, along with the songs originally envisioned for performance, suitable hymns from the Public Domain are suggested in this script.

Please Note: Neither Austin House Publishing nor Martha Ford Fry hold the Performance or Publishing Rights to any song suggested in this Play Script. It is the responsibility of any Producer to obtain Performance Rights for any and all songs used that are not in the Public Domain. Song titles in this Play Script are merely suggestions for those wishing to stage this Play as a Musical.

First Published in 2012
By Austin House Publishing
McDonough, Georgia

All Rights Reserved

Copyright by Martha Ford Fry, 2012

Martha Ford Fry is hereby identified as author of this
Work in accordance with Section 77 of the Copyright,
Designs, and Patents Act 1988

All rights whatsoever in this play are strictly reserved and professional and amateur applications for permission to perform it, etc. must be made in advance, before rehearsals begin, to Austin House Publishing, 318 Dylan Way, McDonough, GA 30252.

This book is sold subject to the condition that it shall not, by way of trade or otherwise, be lent, resold, hired out or otherwise circulated without the publisher's prior consent in any form of binding or cover other than that which it is published and without a similar condition including this condition being imposed on the subsequent purchaser.

ISBN-13: 978-0615667133
ISBN-10: 0615667139

SOMEBODY SAY "GLORY"

"He truly is no fool who gives what he cannot keep to gain what he cannot lose".

Jim Elliot

a play in two acts

by

Martha Ford Fry

Featuring Musical Suggestions

SOMEBODY SAY GLORY - Martha Ford Fry

CHARACTERS

NATE SAINT	Missionary pilot
MARJ SAINT	Nate's wife
JIM ELLIOT	Missionary
BETTY ELLIOT/GIKARI	Jim's wife
ED MCCULLY	Missionary
MARILOU MCCULLY	Ed's wife
PETE FLEMING	Missionary
OLIVE FLEMING	Pete's wife
ROGER YOUDERIAN	Missionary
BARB YOUDERIAN	Roger's wife
MINCAYE	Auca Indian warrior
KIMO	Auca Indian warrior
GIKITA	Auca Indian warrior
NAENKIWI/GEORGE	Auca Indian warrior
RACHEL SAINT/NIMU	Missionary, Nate's sister
DAYUMA	Auca Indian woman
AKAWO	Dayuma's mother
MINTAKA	Dayuma's aunt
GIMARI	Dayuma's younger sister
MATT MCCULLY	Ed and Marilou McCully's grown son
STEVE SAINT	Nate and Marj Saint's grown son

SOMEBODY SAY GLORY – Martha Ford Fry

SOMEBODY SAY GLORY - Martha Ford Fry

SCENES

ACT I

Scene 1	Introductions
Scene 2	Savages
Scene 3	The Mission
Scene 4	Doubts
Scene 5	Gifts
Scene 6	Palm Beach
Scene 7	Disaster
Scene 8	The Storm

ACT II

Scene 1	To Stay or to Go
Scene 2	A Woman's Touch
Scene 3	Salvation
Scene 4	God Followers
Scene 5	Trouble
Scene 6	Reconciliation

SOMEBODY SAY GLORY - Martha Ford Fry

ACT I

SCENE ONE

INTRODUCTIONS

Scene:

The stage is dark and empty.

(*Enter* Olive. *Spotlight up. She knits a pair of argyle socks.*)

Olive (*to Audience*) These argyle socks? Oh, they're a gift for the Greek. You know - Pete Fleming. I call him The Greek because that's what he's studying at the University of Washington. He's quite the scholar, actually. One day I expect him to be a professor of literature somewhere. I've had a unique window on Pete's life. We grew up together in the same Brethren congregation in Seattle. He's three years older, so we've run in slightly different circles. Still, I've watched him grow from the kid who squirmed in his seat during service to a man who gave up ice skating so he would have more time to study the Bible. Do you think he'll ever think of me as more than just one of the teenyboppers from the youth group?

(Olive *holds up the knitting.*)

Olive (*Continues*) Maybe these will get me a response to that question.

(*Spotlight down. Exit* Olive. *Enter* Pete *holding a gift box. Spotlight up.*)

Pete (*to Audience*) It's from Olive Ainslie – a girl back home.

(Pete *opens box and pulls out a pair of argyle socks.*)

Pete (*Continues*) Argyle socks. And, I bet she knit them herself. She's such a sweet girl. I just fear she's expecting more from me than I can give. I believe Jim Elliot's right – exploring remote jungle regions must be done by single men. Family responsibilities affect judgment, and we have to be free to risk everything for Christ right now. Still, I can't deny she's peaked my interest of late. I mean, I've known her all her life – my mother threw the baby shower when Mrs. Ainslie was expecting Olive. But something changed after she came back from a summer job counseling kids at Camp Imadene on Vancouver Island. Now she talks about people's need for God. And when she does, her face reflects the depth of her soul's concern. I think the young girl may be turning into a woman of God.

(*Pause.*)

Pete (*Decisively*) I should write her.

(*Pause.*)

Pete *(Continues in a tone of justification)* Isn't that the polite thing to do? After all, I need to thank her for the socks.

(Spotlight down. Exit Pete. Enter Marj holding an 8 ½ x 11 manila envelope, addressed as if it has been mailed. Spotlight up.)

Marj *(To Audience)* The strangest thing just happened. A girlfriend called me down to her room here in nurses' housing. Her mother sent her this large envelope of letters and pictures of a family friend – Nate Saint's his name.

*(**Marj** holds up the envelope.)*

Marj *(Continues)* Joanna has three sisters, and her mother is hoping that one of them will marry Nate. But she wants me to read the letters – she doesn't think he's meant for any of them. She thinks I'll marry him. What do you think of that? I'd never even heard the man's name before today.

(Pause.)

Marj *(Continues, curiously)* But, I've got to tell you, I've never heard a man my age express feelings of love and service for God like Nate has in these letters.

(Marj pulls out a picture of a young man in a flight uniform and shows it to the audience.)

Marj *(Continues, lightheartedly)* And, he's easy on the eyes, too.

(Spotlight down. Exit Marj. Enter Nate in flight uniform. Spotlight up.)

Nate *(To Audience)* Marjorie Farris and I have been friends now for about three years. Just friends, I've actually been dating another girl. Funny thing about being friends with a girl. It takes a lot of the pressure off – you can talk without always feeling like you've got to impress. Last Saturday night, we were having one of our talks, and she told me about going down to the Church of the Open Door. A missionary was speaking, the first missionary Marj had ever seen in person. At the altar call, she walked down, all the way from the third balcony, and fell on her knees. She told God that she wanted His will for her life at any cost. I'm seeing Marj in a different light this morning. I believe that she's the girl that God's been preparing to be my wife.

(Pulls out a small box and opens it, flashing an engagement ring.)

Nate *(Continues, confidently)* And, if it's God's will, as far as I'm concerned, it's all over except for the hardware!

(Spotlight down. Exit Nate. Enter Betty. Spotlight up.)

Betty *(To Audience)* Well, tonight was a first. Jim Elliot took me for a stroll – and we ended up walking through the cemetery. Although, in all fairness to him, he made it clear from the onset that this was not a date. I about got my head bit off when I mentioned we might go for an ice cream. Jim's sworn off ice cream as he prepares for the mission field. What does ice cream have to do with missions, you ask – don't feel silly, I asked him the same thing. His answer: 'Foreign mission fields are no holidays.' If he doesn't discipline himself now, he's worried that jungle life may overwhelm him. So, he's set out to prepare his body as well as his soul. He's determined not to let anything interfere with his mission to preach the Gospel. And, that includes any cravings for a double dip of rocky road.

(Spotlight down. Exit Betty. *Enter* Jim. *Spotlight up.)*

Jim *(To Audience)* I've been a bit embarrassed about my feelings for Betty Howard – especially after all the fuss I've made about being like the Apostle Paul and remaining single. Even though my family doesn't think she suits me, when we are alone together, we get along so well. And Betty is so committed to allowing God to lead her life. She won't even let me hold her hand. 'I'm not mine to give you,' she tells me. Her feelings mirror my own as does her passion for missions. Few single women would come to Ecuador as missionaries as Dorothy and Betty have done. Especially, since raising their own support is so difficult because women are not allowed to speak in front of Brethren congregations. So, despite my own protests about marriage, I believe that God has given me the green light to marry Betty. I'm going to ask her tonight.

(Spotlight down, Exit Jim. *Enter* Roger. *Spotlight up.)*

Roger *(To Audience)* Can I tell you about Barbara Orton? She's just the greatest gal I've ever known – met her right here in Minneapolis on the Northwestern campus. We're both majoring in Christian education and missionary medicine. And, like me, she feels led to missionary service. We've talked about the Gospel Missionary Union – even though we both know that means pioneer missions. But going to a remote region doesn't seem to scare her, and her knack for languages could certainly benefit us – both in learning to communicate with the people and with getting the Bible translated. Oh, did I actually say that – 'benefit US'? Well, you know what the Good Book says – what comes out of the mouth, comes from the heart. I'm seeing her tonight. Don't have a ring,

(Pulls out an old pocket watch from his pocket.)

Roger *(Continues)* but I can give her this old watch – it's the most valuable thing I own. And more practical than a ring, right?

(Spotlight down. Exit Roger. *Enter* Barb. *Spotlight up.)*

Barb *(To Audience, displaying a pocket watch)* Roger Youderian gave me this old pocket watch this evening, asked me to keep time for him. It was his way of proposing. How could I resist? I fell in love with Roger the first time I saw him walk across the campus at Northwestern. What a striking figure he cut in his uniform. He had just been discharged from the paratroops.

(Pause.)

Barb *(Continues)* Now, I know what some of you girls are thinking - he should have given me a ring; he could have delivered a more romantic proposal. But, truth be known, no ring could hold more value. You've got to know Roger – he's a rugged man, born and raised in central Montana. He contracted polio when he was only nine, but he wouldn't let the disease cripple him permanently. By the time he was in high school, he was able to join the basketball team. And, you've got to know the watch. He got this watch when he worked as a ranch hand. He took it with him to Europe – was on him when he fought at the Battle of the Bulge, and he used it when he was a member of Eisenhower's honor guard. It's not something he would part with lightly. And when he gave it to me, the words came from his heart – and that, my friends, holds a romance all its own.

>*(Spotlight down. Exit* Barb*. Enter* Marilou *wearing a pair of pedal pushers, a plain cotton blouse, and a heavy, dowdy-looking coat. Spotlight up.)*

Marilou *(To Audience)* Boy, am I beat! We had an all-day sports competition for the youth group at church. Since I'm on staff, I had to attend. It wouldn't have been bad except it had been snowing for days, and I had to walk to church. And, wouldn't you know it, my best friend Martha had invited Ed McCully to come down and join us. He wrestles at Wheaton, and Martha thought he would enjoy our home-grown games. He dove right in and soon had made friends with just about everybody. A real cut-up he was. I guess I shouldn't be surprised – he is president of his class. And, while he's definitely good-looking, I think it's his infectious personality that's made him one of the most popular students on Wheaton's campus.

>*(Pause.)*

Marilou *(Continues)* Martha's hoping he'll write her after he returns to school. I don't know why I'm worried about it – while the other girls were quite noticeable in their fancy dresses,

>*(Motions towards her clothes.)*

Marilou *(Continues)* I can't imagine that I made any kind of impression on him.

>*(Spotlight down. Exit* Marilou*. Enter* Ed *holding a Bible. Spotlight up.)*

Ed *(To Audience)* My friend Martha invited me out to a youth sports competition at her church. Martha knows I love any kind of sports activity. Turnout was good, despite the snow. I think the world of Martha, but she had a friend with her – Marilou Hobolth. I just can't get my mind off of her. You should have seen her out there. While all the other girls were dressed up in these silly fancy dresses, Marilou was dressed to play. Even after trudging through the snow to get to the church, she was the most beautiful girl in the place.

>*(Ed pulls out an envelope from the Bible.)*

Ed *(Continues)* Well, I've decided to write her. Don't know if she'll take a fancy to me after she's read this, however.

>   *(Pause.)*

Ed *(Continues)* When I met her, I was going to be a lawyer. But, lately I've been spending my free time studying the Bible, and each night the Lord seems to get hold of me a little more. On the way home from work yesterday, I took a long walk and came to a decision. I don't know where He will lead, maybe He'll send me someplace where they've never heard the name of Jesus; but, that's where I'll go. And, I think Marilou may just be the gal God has in mind to take the journey with me.

>   *(Pause. Music begins.)*

Ed *(Continues)* That may seem a bit impulsive, but this is what God has placed on my heart - If there's nothing to this business of eternal life we might as well lose everything in one crack and throw our present life away anyway. But if there *is* something to it, then everything else the Lord says must hold true likewise, and I have no choice but to live a life of reckless abandon for Him.

Song Suggestions:

Lifesong. Words and Music by John Mark Hall. (Performance Rights Required)

All to Jesus I Surrender. (Public Domain)

>   FADE OUT

ACT I

SCENE TWO

SAVAGES

Scene:

Jungle in Ecuador, with clearing just left of center stage.

(Enter Mincaye and Dayuma, running until they reach clearing.)

Mincaye Dayuma! Where are you going?

Dayuma I must find a place to hide.

Mincaye Hide from what?

Dayuma Do not pretend you do not know what is happening! Moipa has speared my father. He will soon die. My mother has promised to bury me with him.

Dayuma's Father *(Cries heard offstage)* Dayuma! Dayuma!

Dayuma I cannot live with our people any longer. I must leave the jungle and find a place where I can be safe.

Mincaye Dayuma, you are speaking as a silly girl. How will you leave the jungle? We are one with the jungle. It provides our very source of life!

Dayuma Life! You call this life! They spear us today, and then we spear them tomorrow. Do you know what the Quechua up river call us? AUCA! They call us Auca, because we live like savages. Even now, we number only about 50 tribesmen – all the rest dead, dead from spearing.

Mincaye We spear to survive. By spearing, we prove our superiority, our strength. Running away just shows weakness.

Dayuma It may be weakness, but I would rather be weak than dead. Nimu, my precious baby sister, has been macheted to death and, now, my own family seeks to kill me as well. What future do I have here in the jungle?

Dayuma's Father *(Cries heard from offstage)* Dayuma! Bring me Dayuma!

Mincaye But, Dayuma, if your father has been speared, you must go to him as he dies.

Dayuma No. I can't go. You know what will happen if I go to him. My own mother will strangle me. She will throw me in the grave with him just so the old man is comforted while he dies. But what about comfort for me? Who will comfort me as my mother kills me?

Mincaye But, Dayuma, your father is weak. He will not be able to climb the Great Boa by himself. If he fails to climb and falls back to earth, he will become a termite. You must help him climb the Great Boa.

Dayuma No, Mincaye. I don't want to die. My father has lived a life of spearing. He has viciously killed many men – not just men, but women and children. I think the Quechua are right – we are savages, we are Auca. Now, it's true, my father is dying – dying by the spear that has become more precious to him than his own children. Well, I am not willing to die with him.

Mincaye And, what do you intend to do? Do you think you can hunt meat or make manioc in the jungle on your own? Do you think you can survive the spears of our enemies without the tribe to protect you?

Dayuma And, will the tribe protect me from my own mother and father? No.

Mincaye And, so where will you go, clever girl? Where will you go with only nuts and berries to survive?

Dayuma I'll, I'll ….

> *(Pause.)*

Dayuma *(Continues, decisively)* I am going to go to the foreigners. If the foreigners are doing well, maybe they will protect me.

Mincaye You are a foolish, foolish girl. The foreigners will kill you.

Dayuma Perhaps they will. They will either help me, or they will kill me. But, if I stay with the tribe, I am sure to be killed.

Dayuma's Father *(Cries heard offstage)* Bring me Dayuma! Dayuma! Dayuma!

> *(Fearfully looking at* Mincaye, *and then turning away,* Dayuma *runs across stage with her eyes closed.)*

Dayuma *(Shouting)* Help me! Help me!

> *(Enter* Rachel Saint. Dayuma *runs into her.* Rachel *grabs* Dayuma*'s arms to stop her.)*

Rachel Come here child! What's wrong?

Dayuma Help me! Oh, please help me!

SOMEBODY SAY GLORY – Martha Ford Fry

Rachel I don't understand a word you are saying. Where did you come from?

>(Dayuma *looks back to the jungle.* Mincaye *hides behind a tree.* Rachel *looks but does not see him.)*

Dayuma Help me! Help me!

>(Dayuma *looks back to the jungle again.)*

Rachel Are you alone, child? Are there others? Is someone chasing you?

Dayuma Help me! Please help me!

>(Dayuma *looks back to the jungle.* Mincaye *stays hidden, watching.* Rachel *tugs on* Dayuma*'s arm, motioning for her to follow her.)*

Rachel Come, let's go to the house and find you some clothes.

>(Dayuma *hesitates, looking back momentarily in the direction of* Mincaye. Rachel *looks but does not see* Mincaye.*)*

Rachel Come, come. You are safe in this place. Ven conmigo. Ven conmigo.

>(Dayuma *looks back once again at* Mincaye. Dayuma *breaks free from* Rachel*'s hold and runs off stage.* Rachel *calls after her.)*

Rachel Ven conmigo

Song Suggestions:

Does Anybody Hear Her? Words and Music by John Mark Hall (Performance Rights Required)

Rescue the Perishing. Words by Frances Jane Crosby and Music by William Howard Doane (Public Domain)

All Because We Do Love Them. Words and Music by Daniel O. Teasley (Public Domain)

>(*Enter* Dayuma. Rachel *picks up a blanket from the ground and puts it around her. With* Rachel*'s hands on* Dayuma*'s shoulders, guiding her, moving towards stage right.* Rachel *begins singing the refrain.* Rachel *stops just before leaving the stage and looks back at* Mincaye, *who is still behind a tree in the jungle. Exit* Mincaye. Rachel *finishes singing the refrain. Exit* Rachel *and* Dayuma.*)*

FADE OUT

ACT I

SCENE THREE

THE MISSION

Scene:

Kitchen of Saint home at Shell Mera, Ecuador.

>(Jim, Pete, *and* Ed *peruse large aerial map on kitchen table. Enter* Nate *and* Roger.*)*

Nate Hey, guys. I want you to meet Roger Youderian. He and his wife Barbara have made contact with the Ashuara tribe.

>(Men *extend their hands to* Roger.*)*

Nate *(Continues)* Roger has really made progress in forming bonds with the Ashuara by providing medical supplies. This guy trekked 50 miles through the mud just to get a load of penicillin into a remote jungle village. He staved off a flu epidemic single handedly and earned the tribe's respect in the process.

Roger I don't know if I would go that far.

Jim So, what brings you to Shell Mera?

Roger Nate believes we need a medical clinic up here. Jungle medicine techniques are not enough to treat some of the more serious illnesses and injuries. After being out in the field for a while, I think he's right. So, I agreed to come up here and help him build a clinic.

Nate *(To Roger)* I do need help with the clinic, but I've got another reason for asking you up here this weekend, Roger.

Nate *(Continues, addressing all the men)* I think we ought to let Roger in on our operation, guys. He's a former paratrooper, seen serious action. He fought in the Battle of the Bulge and participated in the Rhine Jump. Nothing riles him. He's got nerves of steel and has had serious survival training.

Jim Well, if you think he ought to be brought in, Nate, I guess it's alright by me. Just so he knows the risks.

Nate He's been down here long enough. He knows the risks.

>*(Pause.)*

Nate *(Continues, speaking to Roger)* It's the Aucas, Roger. We're hashing out a plan to contact these people. But, we've got to keep this thing quiet. You know the general edict from all our missionary organizations has been "no Auca engagement". However, we really believe that the time is now.

Ed The recent Auca attacks on oil company outposts have just increased the retaliatory attacks by the oil company security forces.

Jim At some point, the oil companies are going to put significant pressure on the government to go in with military force and just wipe out the tribe. We can't sit by and let that happen.

Roger And you think you will be able to locate the Aucas and make peaceful contact? From what little I know of the tribe, they appear to be extremely nomadic and, how should I say it, not very hospitable.

Ed Well, as to the first part of your question, we've already found them. Here.

(Points to a spot on the map.)

Ed *(Continues)* Here is where Nate and I found the huts. One large one, surrounded by five or six smaller, thatched huts. It's near the Curaray, but the clearing is carved out of an intensely thick jungle area. Actually, it's only about a 15 minute flight from where I'm stationed in Arajuno.

Pete From what we've learned about the Aucas from the Quechua, everything points to this being an Auca settlement. And you're right, they are nomadic, but they seem to only move camp when seriously threatened. That's one reason this needs to happen quickly. If they get attacked – whether by the military, oil company security, or another tribe - they will most likely burn this village and retreat further into the jungle. Who knows when we'll be able to find them again?

Nate And, as for your second concern, I've got an idea on how to make a safe first contact. The plan is to offer them gifts – a type of peace offering. Let them know we are friendly and have things of value to share.

Roger And, how do you propose that we give them those gifts without endangering ourselves?

Nate Well, actually, I've been thinking about that for quite a while. When I was in college I developed a concept using a pencil at the end of a string.

(Nate ties a wooden #2 pencil to the end of a string and dangles it, moving his hand in circles until the pencil hangs still.)

Nate As you draw the string into tighter and tighter circles, the pencil eventually hangs nearly perfectly still.

SOMEBODY SAY GLORY - Martha Ford Fry

Jim Even though your hand is still making circles.

Nate Correct. And, I believe the same premise will work using a bucket at the end of a rope from the Piper. As the plane makes increasingly tighter circles, the bucket should eventually hang still over the target area, allowing us to drop gifts safely.

Jim And, with more precision and less risk of damage than simply tossing a package out of the plane into the tribe's encampment.

Nate Right here…

(Pointing to the map)

Nate *(Continues)* There's a sandbar that I think is long enough to allow for a safe landing of the Piper.

Roger It looks to be about three miles from the village.

Ed That's about how we figured it as well. Once we've made it clear that we've come in peace, we can set up a primitive base camp to make face to face contact.

(Pete looks a little worried.)

Jim You O.K., Pete?

Pete This is all exciting stuff, I'm just not sure that this is where God wants me right now. Olive and I have just begun our work in Puyupugo.

Jim And, we all respect that. It's your decision.

Pete I just want to be where God wants me to be and not be enticed by all the excitement.

(Music begins.)

Nate I think we all feel that way. We've agreed to go wherever God leads us. If that's to the Aucas, and I believe it is, then God's got to go with us if we're going to survive.

(Ed looks upward.)

Song Suggestions:

In Me. Words and Music by John Mark Hall (Performance Rights Required.)

Trust and Obey. Words by John H. Sammis and Music by Daniel Brink Towner (Public Domain)

FADE OUT

SOMEBODY SAY GLORY – Martha Ford Fry

ACT I

SCENE FOUR

DOUBTS

Scene:

Rudimentary church in jungle in Ecuador. Chairs are lined in rows, backs to the audience and facing a low platform with a pulpit.

> *(Enter* Roger *and* Barb, *dressed in 1950s Sunday best and carrying Bibles.)*

Roger I don't want to talk to the others about my doubts today, Barb. Let's just keep this between you and me for now.

Barb I'll do whatever you want, Roger, you know that. But I think if you've really decided to go back to the States, you ought to speak to someone about it before you formally submit the paperwork. You know Ralph Stuck would give you wise counsel.

Roger I know he would, Barb. But, I guess it's that pride thing. Do I really want anyone to know that I've allowed myself to get so discouraged? That I'm ready to give up? The others have just made so much progress with their tribes here in the Oriente. I have just failed the Ashuara so terribly.

Barb How do you know that they've had such an easy time of it? That they haven't had the same frustrations, felt like they were at the end of their ropes? Maybe they are more like you than you think – maybe, because of their own pride, they only confide in their wives.

> *(Enter* Ed *and* Marilou.*)*

Ed Isn't this a great day, Roger?

> *(*Roger *nods and smiles. The two couples shake hands.)*

Ed Only one thing I know could make it better – if we had some natives here worshipping with us. But, it won't be long now, I'm sure. I think some of the Quechua we've been working with will soon be ready to come and study God's Word with us.

> *(*Ed *and* Marilou *take their seats in the church. Enter* Pete *and* Olive.*)*

Pete How's it going Roger?

> *(*Roger *nods and shakes his hand.)*

Barb How're you feeling, Olive?

SOMEBODY SAY GLORY - Martha Ford Fry

Olive Much better, thanks. Each day seems to get a little easier for me here. Of course, I don't think Puypunga will ever feel like Seattle.

Pete No, but would we ever see the response to the gospel in Seattle that we are seeing in Puypunga? It's just amazing how open this tribe is to learning about God. I'm so excited about the work there, I can hardly wait to get up in the morning and see what God will do next!

Olive Well, if I don't go in and sit down, what you may be doing next is carrying me back home.

Pete Yeah, I better get her off her feet. We'll see you inside.

> (Pete *and* Olive *take their seats in the church and speak to* Ed *and* Marilou *(unheard). Enter* Nate *and* Marj *and greet* Roger *and* Barb.)

Nate Wow, Roger! What a week this has been, huh? I think I've spent more time in the cockpit than on terra firma. But, it's such a privilege to be able to keep the supplies rolling out to you guys in the jungle.

> (Nate *and* Marj *take their seats and talk to the others in the church (unheard). Enter* Jim *and* Betty *and greet* Roger *and* Barb.)

Jim Hey, brother! Did you hear? Some Quechua invited us to a local festival the other evening. Olive was still too sick to go, but Pete, Betty, Dorothy, and I went. The tribe just accepted us as one of their own. It was amazing.

> (Betty *sits down.* Jim *goes to the pulpit and opens his Bible.*)

Roger *(To Barb)* Somehow I don't get the impression that any of these guys are discouraged.

Barb Come on. Jim's about ready to start.

> (Roger *and* Barb *go in and take seats on the aisle. Music begins.*)

Jim Let's turn to Nehemiah. God had put a great mission in the heart of Nehemiah, one that he would have to keep secret for a time.

> (Jim *continues unheard. Lights dim. Spotlight on* Roger *as he stands up unnoticed.* Roger *moves throughout the church, singing first verse to the participants unnoticed.*)

Song Suggestions:

Stained Glass Masquerade. Words and Music by John Mark Hall and Nichole Nordeman

God of Grace and God of Glory. Words by Harry Emerson Fosdick; Music by John Hughes (Public Domain)

>**Director's Note:** This song has no refrain, but the lines "Grant us wisdom, grant us courage…" can be repeated and used where the refrain is noted.

Director's Note: Songs should be divided up by verses with the following actions inserted between each verse sung.

>*(*Roger *kneels at the front of the pulpit. Spotlight on* Barb *as she stands up and moves through the church, singing the first lines of the second verse to the congregation, unnoticed.)*

>*(*Roger *rises and begins singing the refrain to the congregation with* Barb*.)*

>*(*All *stand up in their seats and bows their heads.* Roger *sings the end of the second verse.)*

>*(*Barb *and* Roger *fall to their knees in prayer. As music plays,* Two Dancers *wearing masquerade masks appear to stage right.* Barb *and* Roger *both look up and sing refrain together.* Dancers *continue.)*

>*(Music continues to play.* Jim *and* Betty *leave the church. Others stand frozen as stage lights dim and spotlight hits* Jim *and* Betty *at front of stage right.)*

Betty Jim, we were wrong to be drinking at that fiesta. And, under no circumstances should we have allowed Dorothy to dance with the men of the tribe.

Jim Betty, you can't continue to let this eat away at you. This was the first time any non-native has ever been asked to participate in the tribal fiesta. It was an important step, and we didn't need to offend them by refusing their hospitality. Besides, we only had a few sips of alcohol. It's not like we were drunk.

Betty But what if we irreparably damaged our testimony with that tribe – or the testimony of other missionaries they may come in contact with? I won't be able to live with myself if that happens.

>*(Exit* Jim *and* Betty*, escorted by* Dancers*, as music continues.* Pete *and* Olive *walk to front of stage right and into spotlight.)*

Pete Are you really feeling alright?

Olive I feel more emotionally sick right now than physically sick. I just don't understand God's plan for us, Pete.

Pete I know, but we have to trust God, maybe now more than ever.

Olive But how could God call you to a place where I can't tolerate the climate and I can't keep the food down? And, it's not enough for me to be sick all the time, now we've had not one, but two miscarriages. Does obedience mean I will never know the joy of being a mother?

> *(Exit* Pete *and* Olive, *escorted by* Dancers. *Spotlight on* Roger *and* Barb *as they sing the third verse. Music continues. Lights dim.* Roger *and* Barb *freeze.* Marilou *and* Ed *walk into spotlight on stage right.)*

Marilou I'm scared, Ed. I really don't want you heading out with Nate tomorrow.

Ed I know, Marilou. But I need to help him scout the Auca territory. It's just too difficult for him to do it alone.

Marilou Scout the territory? I think the Aucas are already scouting us! The Quechua don't even want to come downriver to help me any longer because they have seen Aucas come right up to our fence. What if they attack me, or worse, one of the boys and you're not there?

> *(Exit* Ed *and* Marilou, *escorted by the* Dancers. Nate *and* Marj *enter spotlight at front of stage right.)*

Nate We almost got caught yesterday. Marion Stuck came up to the house. When she couldn't find you, she came out to the workshop. I think I intercepted her before she saw me working on the model planes, but it was still too close for my comfort.

Marj Even if she did see the models, she probably would have assumed they were gifts for the children.

Nate Still, I don't like having to be so secretive. It's against my nature. I know we are called to reach the Aucas for Christ, but in order to do so we lie to our families, our friends, our co-laborers here. We even lie to our mission agencies who have told us not to contact the Aucas. It makes me uneasy not to be truthful with people.

> *(Exit* Nate *and* Marj, *escorted by the* Dancers. Roger *and* Barb *walk over to their seats and pick up their Bibles.* Roger *sings final verse and refrain and then Exit* Roger *and* Barb, *escorted by* Dancers.*)*

FADE OUT

SOMEBODY SAY GLORY - Martha Ford Fry

ACT I

SCENE FIVE

GIFTS

Scene:

Saint home in Shell Mera, Ecuador. Kitchen area is stage right, living room area stage left, fireplace at far stage left.

> *(Jim, Ed, Pete, and Nate are at the kitchen table, coloring photographs. Enter Betty and Marj.)*

Marj What's going on? You all seem so engrossed.

Nate Just a little prep work for our next gift drop.

> *(Nate holds up a black and white photograph, partially colored with markers.)*

Marj You're giving them photographs of yourselves? I think they might prefer more cooking pots and machetes.

Jim *(Ignoring Marj's attempt at humor.)* We need them to become familiar with our faces.

> *(Jim stands and shows his photograph to Betty.)*

Jim See, we're holding the gifts that they have sent back to us in the photos. Hopefully, when they see us in person, they will recognize our faces from the photographs and realize we've been the ones dropping the gifts.

> *(Betty takes the photograph and examines it.)*

Betty You've got little planes etched in the corners?

Ed To make sure that they associate us with the plane. And, look at this, girls, look what Nate's put together.

> *(Ed pulls a yellow wooden toy plane from underneath the table.)*

Ed He made models of the Piper. This one I'm going to post outside our house in Arajuno. If the Auca are venturing out as far as the outpost – as the Quechua seem to think they are, we're hoping they'll tie it all together - the plane with the gifts and the plane at the house.

Marj But why are you coloring the photos?

Nate The Aucas are not familiar with photographs. We want to make the photos look as much like what they'll see when they meet us.

Pete They won't see us in black and white, so we're coloring them in.

Marj So, I guess we're getting close to attempting a face-to-face meeting.

Nate I think it's fair to say, it'll happen soon. The bucket drops have been even more successful than we could have hoped for – we never dreamt they would actually start sending presents back.

> (Betty *motions* Marj *to join her in the living room. They sit and start talking to each other (unheard).* Jim, Ed, Pete, *and* Nate *continue to talk to each other. Excited, they don't notice the women's departure.)*

Ed I must admit, opening that canvas bag up and finding a live parrot was a bit disconcerting.

Pete But, could we have received better evidence that the Aucas are ready for a peaceful meeting?

Nate Absolutely not. God has taken our prayers and our willingness to go and is opening the hearts of the Aucas – I'm sure of it. God has said that every tribe will be represented in heaven, and now, we are witnesses to His preparing a way for the Aucas to receive the gospel.

Ed It does make you wonder –

Song Suggestions:

What if His People Prayed. Words and Music by John Mark Hall (Performance Rights Required.)

We Rest on Thee. Words by Edith G. Cherry and Music by Jean Sibelius (Public Domain)

Director's Note: The song in this scene can be cut in its entirety if there is an issue regarding performance time. If the song is cut or if the hymn is used, the previous line by "Ed" should be cut as well.

> (Marj *and* Betty *rejoin the men in the kitchen area.)*

Nate And one day, Auca warriors will be counted among the people called by His name. Marj, you should have seen them today. They had actually built a platform high in one of the trees near the village. An Auca man was waiting up there, waving us towards the drop point. It was almost like they were saying "Here we are! Don't fly by! Don't miss us!"

Marj With things going so well, it does seem that going in would be the next step.

Jim Yep, and very soon. Probably right after Christmas, we'll fly supplies in to build an outpost on the sandbar. It's got enough room to land the Piper, and it's within walking distance to the village.

Nate We've given it the code name "Palm Beach".

> (Betty *looks worriedly at* Marj, *who looks briefly at the ground. As* Betty *looks back at the guys;* Marj *looks back at Betty.*)

Betty You're all going to go in and set up this camp?

Nate That's the plan!

Jim Why? What did you think we'd be doing?

Betty I don't know.

> (Betty *looks at* Marj *again, but* Marj *looks down at the floor.*)

Betty *(Continues)* I just don't think five men... I don't think it's wise.

Pete What do you mean?

Betty The Aucas have already been attacked numerous times by the military and by the oil company security forces. If all five of you go in there – well, I just don't see how you are going to appear any different, at least in the eyes of the Auca, than those men? And those attempts at contact have always resulted in bloodshed.

> *(Silence.)*

Betty *(Continues, hesitantly)* I just think, I just think…

> *(Pause.)*

Betty *(Continues, now forcibly)* I just think it would be better if Jim and Valerie and I went down the river in a canoe. Five men coming in on a flying contraption – it looks like an invasion. They are going to feel threatened, and Aucas don't respond well when they sense danger. But, there's certainly no way they could view a man and his family, approaching in a simple canoe, unarmed, as a threat.

Jim That's not a bad idea, fellas. I'd be up for it.

(Silence. All look at Nate.)

Nate *(Defiantly)* No. The men are going in. On the plane.

                                                         FADE OUT

ACT I

SCENE SIX

PALM BEACH

Scene:

A sandbar in the jungle in Ecuador.

> (*Jim and* Roger *put up a canvas shade.* Pete *mans a grill, cooking hamburgers. Enter* Nate *and* Ed, *carrying boxes of supplies. The yellow wing of the Piper is visible at stage left.*)

Nate Well, I think that's the last of it for this trip. How's it going?

Jim Well, we've got shade now, and the treehouse…

> (*Jim walks over and pats the trunk of a tall palm tree.*)

Jim *(Continues)*…worked out great. I think we all slept like babies up there.

Pete How are the girls doing?

Nate They're doing great.

Roger I knew Barb would hold up. She's used to my being gone for long periods of time, but I'll still be glad to see her and Beth and Jerry when I fly out of here with you on Sunday.

Pete How about some burgers? I think these are just about done. There's some lemonade over there if you're thirsty.

> (*Jim holds up a pitcher of lemonade.*)

Jim Yea, it's warm, but at least it's wet.

> (*Each of the men grab a burger,* Jim *pours lemonade into five mason jars. They all then sit around the fire.*)

Nate Now, I guess we just have to wait and see if we get some visitors.

Pete Well, they certainly must know we're here by now. Jim and I have been shouting Auca phrases from the river bank all day long.

Nate Thank God for Dayuma. I don't know how we would have communicated with them without the phrases we learned from her.

Pete This has definitely been God's doing. We could not have accomplished this on our own.

  (Jim rises to his feet.)

Song Suggestions:

Director's Note: This song can be cut for time purposes.

Glory. Words and Music by Hector Cervantes and John Mark Hall (Performance Permission Required.)

Holy, Holy, Holy. Words by Reginald Heber and Music by John Bacchus Dykes

He Leadeth Me. Words by Joseph Henry Gilmore and Music by William Batchelder Bradbury (Public Domain)

  (Enter Gimari, Naenkiwi, and Mintaka.)

Jim *(Awestruck)* Somebody say Glory! We've got company, gentlemen.

  (Gimari, Naenkiwi, and Mintaka near campsite. Gimari walks over to the plane wing and starts rubbing her hands along it. Nate, Jim, Pete, Ed, and Roger don't take their eyes off of Gimari.)

Gimari Take me to my sister, Dayuma. She is with the foreigners. Take me to her.

  (Nate, Jim, Pete, Ed, and Roger look at each other, bewildered.)

Jim Pete, you have any idea what she's saying?

Pete She's talking too fast, but she's certainly interested in the airplane.

Naenkiwi *(Motioning towards Gimari)* Gimari wants to go in your wood-bee to see her sister. Dayuma is her sister. Take her to her.

  (Pete, Ed, and Roger walk over to Naenkiwi and Mintaka, smiling and nodding their heads.)

Mintaka *(Pointing towards the plane and Gimari)* I want to go, too. Take me to Dayuma.

Roger *(To the other Missionaries)* Any ideas as to what they are saying?

Pete I'm not really sure. They're talking too rapidly for me to catch anything. But, from the way they're acting, it seems like they are offering us the younger girl as a gift.

(Jim gets the model airplane from the shelter. Nate retrieves his camera from one of the boxes of supplies and starts snapping photographs. Naenkiwi takes the model plane from Jim and peers inside, then motions with the model like it is flying.)

Naenkiwi You have the wood bee. Take her to Dayuma.

Jim I think he wants to go for a ride.

Nate Well, maybe I should take him for one.

(Nate hands Ed the camera.)

Nate *(Very slowly, to* Naenkiwi*)* What is your name?

Nate *(Continues, to the other* Missionaries*)* What am I supposed to call him – hey you?

Ed Call him "George". You know – "George of the Jungle."

(Ed takes photos as Nate *walks towards the plane.* Nate *motions for* Naenkiwi *to follow him.)*

Nate O.K. Come on, George – let's go for a ride. Jim, Pete – come help me push the plane out.

(Exit Jim, Pete, Nate, *and* George/Naenkiwi. *The sound of an airplane motor is heard, the yellow wing disappears off stage. Enter* Jim *and* Pete *return to the stage.)*

Jim Well, they're up.

(Mintaka looks at the grill. Pete walks over to her, pulling a small journal from his pocket.)

Pete Would you like one?

(Mintaka looks at Pete, perplexed.)

Pete Do you want a hamburger?

(Mintaka continues to look perplexed. Pete takes a hamburger off the grill and puts it on a bun. Pete takes a bite. Pete prepares a second hamburger and offers it to Mintaka.)

Pete You eat it. Would you like one?

(Mintaka takes the hamburger, looking at it intently, finally taking a bite from it, and chewing decisively.)

SOMEBODY SAY GLORY – Martha Ford Fry

Pete Mmmmm. It's good, isn't it?

>(Pete *rubs his belly.*)

Pete Goooood.

>(*Enter* Nate *and* George/Naenkiwi.)

Nate Wow, that was amazing! The whole tribe came out when they heard the plane. George leaned out and hollered at them. For a minute I thought he was going to go right out the side, he was hanging out so far. But, they definitely saw him. They have to know we are friendly now.

>(Naenkiwi *picks up the model plane and flies it through the air.*)

Naenkiwi Now take Gimari. Take her to her sister Dayuma. If she still lives.

Jim I think he wants to go again.

>(Nate *shakes his head no.*)

Nate No, not today.

Nate *(To the other* Missionaries*)* I need to try to make them understand that we need a clear place to land in the jungle.

Pete I had a hard enough time explaining what a hamburger is; I doubt that I can get them to understand that we need them to build an airstrip.

Jim But you got her to eat it by showing her what to do with it. We'll have to approach the airstrip the same way - we'll just have to show them what we need done.

>(Jim *and* Pete *gather a bunch of sticks from the area.*)

Pete What's the plan?

>(Jim *starts standing the sticks upright in an area of sandy beach.*)

Jim Just put your sticks in the ground like this, like trees.

>(Pete *puts his sticks into the sand, upright.* Jim *walks over and gently takes the plane from* Naenkiwi. *He pretends to land the plane in the middle of the sticks, hopping over each one like he's going to crash the plane.*)

Jim See, no good.

>(Missionaries *start waving their hands as in "no good".*)

SOMEBODY SAY GLORY – Martha Ford Fry

Missionaries No good. No good.

Jim We can't bring the plane in with all these trees.

> *(*Jim *and* Roger *start taking the sticks down.)*

Jim Now, we can land the plane.

> *(*Jim *takes the model plane and pretends to make a safe landing with it.* Missionaries *clap.* George/Naenkiwi *claps.* Nate *puts his arm around* George/Naenkiwi *and the other men try to communicate with him (unheard).* Pete *still holds his journal of Wao phrases.* Ed *stops taking pictures and walks over to* Gimari.*)*

Ed *(To the Missionaries)* I think we should call this one Delilah.

Ed *(Continues, to Gimari)* Does that name suit you? Delilah.

> *(*Ed *pulls a photograph out of his shirt pocket and shows it to* Gimari.*)*

Ed This is Dayuma. Dayuma is Auca.

> *(*Gimari *takes the photo out of his hand and shows it to* Mintaka.*)*

Gimari *(To* Mintaka*)* It is Dayuma. He must have eaten her.

> *(*Mintaka *looks at the* Missionaries.*)*

Mintaka They do not act like cannibals.

> *(*Mintaka *looks, inquisitively, at the hamburger in her hand.)*

Mintaka *(Continues)* Buuutt, this is not monkey meat.

Gimari I tell you, he pulled this…

> *(*Gimari *waves the photograph.)*

Gimari *(Continues)* the spirit of Dayuma out of his insides.

Mintaka But these foreigners seem different. I sense no fear. I sense no danger.

> *(*Naenkiwi *leaves the* Missionaries *and walks over to* Mintaka *and* Gimari. *The* Missionaries *follow closely behind* Naenkiwi.*)*

Gimari Dayuma is dead! That is why they will not take me with them in the wood bee.

SOMEBODY SAY GLORY – Martha Ford Fry

Naenkiwi I told you they are no different from all the other foreigners. They kill Aucas. Now you have seen for yourself. They have killed and eaten Dayuma. They will kill and eat you. Go back to the village now, Gimari. I cannot protect you here.

(Exit Gimari, *angrily.* Naenkiwi *throws the model plane down and Exits. The* Missionaries *call after them.* Mintaka *sits down by the fire and continues eating her hamburger. The* Missionaries *stop calling out and stand, looking at* Mintaka, *perplexed.)*

                                                                              FADE OUT

ACT I

SCENE SEVEN

DISASTER

Scene:

Jungle in Ecuador.

> *(Enter* Akawo *from stage right. Enter* Gimari *and* Naenkiwi *from stage left, meeting at center stage.)*

Akawo Did you find the foreigners? Do they know of Dayuma?

Gimari We found the foreigners. They know Dayuma. They hold her spirit.

Naenkiwi *(To* Akawo*)* Silly old woman. Go back to the village. The foreigners have killed Dayuma. And they will kill you.

Akawo Dayuma is dead? How do you know this?

Naenkiwi I tell you. They are bad foreigners. They attacked us and tried to kill us. Now, go back to the village or I will return and kill the foreigners myself.

Akawo No, you go to the village, Naenkiwi. You tend to your wives and children and leave my daughter alone. Has not her brother Nampa already told you that she will not become another wife for you?

Gimari Naenkiwi tells the truth, Mother. One of the foreigners pulled Dayuma's spirit out of his insides. Then they attacked us. If Naenkiwi had not gone with me, surely I would have died.

Akawo You are young. You do not know. I will wait for Mintaka. We will go to the Curaray together, and I will see for myself.

> *(Enter* Gikita *and* Mincaye.*)*

Gikita *(To* Akawo*)* Well, have you seen the foreigners? Are you leaving the village to go with them, you silly old woman?

Gimari Tell her not to go, Gikita. They are bad foreigners. They will kill us.

Naenkiwi They have killed Dayuma, and I am sure other Waodani.

Gikata Then, let's go and make spears. We will go to the beach and kill the foreigners.

(The Men *gather up wood poles, sit down and start carving notches in the poles and filing down the ends. Enter* Mintaka.*)*

Mintaka Akawo, what is going on here? I thought you were to join us with the foreigners. I waited long into the night, but you never came.

Gikita Naenkiwi says the foreigners attacked you. They tried to kill you.

Mintaka Naenkiwi lies. These are good foreigners. They laughed a lot. They shared their meat. They were not like the other foreigners.

Naenkiwi She is an old woman. She speaks nonsense. If we do not kill them now, they will kill us. I tell you the truth.

Mintaka No. They were good to us. Why, Naenkiwi, why are you lying?

Naenkiwi There are only five men now. I tell you, if we do not go kill them now, they will bring more foreigners and they will kill us.

Gikita Naenkiwi is right. Foreigners have come before and all killed Waodani. We must kill these foreigners before they kill us.

Mincaye We must make more spears. We must make more spears fast before they go and get more foreigners to join them.

Gikata Yes, we must go. We must avenge Dayuma and all Waodani who die at the hands of foreigners.

(Exit Men, *spears drawn, yelling.)*

Akawo Come. Let's go high into the jungle and see what happens.

(Exit Women. *Lights fade. Spotlight on* Nate, *kneeling beside a radio transmitter, mouthpiece in hand at stage right.* Roger *and* Pete *are behind him.* Pete *sits reading his book of Wao words, while* Roger *listens.)*

Nate *(Into radio mouthpiece)* We expect visitors for Sunday afternoon service. Pray, girls. Today is the day. Talk to you at 4:30.

Marj *(Voice from offstage)* 10-4. We'll be praying. Talk to you at 4:30. Shell Mera out.

(Turning away from the radio, Nate *shows recognition on his face. Lights come up, very dim, on stage left.* Nate *smiles and waves.* Pete *stands.* Pete *and* Roger *start waving, smiling. Smiles turn to fear and waves to panicked gestures.* Roger *pulls a pistol from belt holster and fires shots into the air.)*

Roger No. No. We are friends.

Aucas *(War cries from offstage)*

> *(Enter* Aucas *with spears drawn. Lights remain dim on* Aucas. *They are visible, but shadowy.)*

Pete No. We are your friends. Friends.

Aucas *(Screaming war cries)*

> *(All freeze just as Auca spears reach the* Missionaries.*)*

FADE OUT

(Sounds of torrential rain.)

SOMEBODY SAY GLORY – Martha Ford Fry

ACT I

SCENE EIGHT

THE STORM

Scene:

Saint home, Shell Mera, Ecuador.

>*(Olive writes in a journal at the kitchen table. Enter Marj from radio room.)*

Marj Still can't raise them on the radio. I sent Kathy over to Johnny Keene's to see if he could contact them. No luck there, either. But, Johnny took off to Arajuno to pick up Marilou and Barb. They should be here shortly.

Olive But what if the men make it to Arajuno and no one is there?

Marj Marilou made sure there was food in the fridge and a note on the door. There's a radio at the house. If they can make it to Arajuno, they'll be fine. Rachel's been visiting at Shandia, so Betty's bringing her here. Betty hasn't let on as to what's been happening. I guess I'm going to have to be the one to talk to Rachel.

>*(Marj notices the journal.)*

Marj *(Continues)* What are you writing?

>*(Olive picks up the journal.)*

Olive Just my prayers and thoughts. I'm afraid I'm not going to remember much if I don't write it down.

>*(As Olive reads, Enter Rachel, Betty, and Marilou. They slowly surround Olive, listening.)*

Olive *(Reading from the journal.)* Someone saw a fire in the jungle last night. Please God, let the men be alright. Please God, bring Pete back. The Quechua work is so important.

>*(Olive looks up from the journal.)*

Olive *(Continues)* No, that's not the truth. I really just want him back for me. I know I'm being selfish. Pete should be the last to survive. Your husbands are fathers. Your children need them. But I waited for him, we did as God asked us to do, we've just started our lives together. He has to come back.

Marj Olive, you can't be so hard on yourself. We went into this knowing there was a possibility that something could go terribly wrong. We just have to keep praying, keep trusting God.

Rachel Those guys are in Auca territory, aren't they?

Marj Yes, Rachel. Nate found an Auca settlement several months ago. On Tuesday, they went out and set up a camp on a nearby sandbar. They made friendly contact on Friday, but now, well, we haven't heard from them since yesterday morning. Nate and Roger were to fly into Arajuno last night to keep the plane safe, but they never arrived.

Olive Where's Barb?

Marilou She flew back out with Johnny. They're going to go fly out over the sandbar and the Auca settlement.

Betty Valerie and I should have gone with Jim. The Aucas would not have felt threatened by a man with his family. I told Nate that. This would not have happened if I had insisted.

Marilou First, we don't know that the men aren't somewhere safe. The storm may have kept them from taking off last night. It may even have interfered with the radio transmission.

Rachel But they all knew the rules – no one was to enter Auca territory.

(Enter Barb, attention shifts to her.)

Barb The news isn't good. We found the plane on the sandbar, but it's been totally stripped. There was no sign of any of the men.

(Music begins.)

Marj I don't understand where God is leading right now, but I do know our emotions cannot overrun our faith. Our husbands turned to God at every step of this mission. And, we must turn to Him now.

(All hold hands and bow their heads in prayer. Lights dim. Spotlight on Marj. Marj separates from the group and looks up to heaven.)

Song Suggestions:

Praise You in the Storm. Words and Music by Bernie Herms and John Mark Hall. (Performance Rights Required)

Does Jesus Care? Words by Frank E. Graeff and Music by Joseph Lincoln Hall (Public Domain)

(Lights dim. All remain visible as they freeze in stances of praise until music ends.)

                 FADE OUT

ACT II

SCENE 1

TO STAY OR TO GO

Scene:

Saint home, Shell Mera, Ecuador

> *(*Marj, Olive, Betty, Marilou, Barb, Dayuma, *and* Rachel *sit at the Saint's kitchen table.)*

Dayuma I don't understand. You are going to leave your men there on the sandbar? In the jungle?

Rachel The men are no longer there, Dayuma. The soldiers merely buried their bodies, their empty shells. We believe in a firm promise from Wangongi, Creator God. He has told us in His carvings that the men, the souls of those men, are now with Him in heaven.

Betty And, that promise is so much more important than what we do with their bodies.

Dayuma I still do not understand.

Rachel We believe death is not the end. It is only a trail. We must choose in this life if we want to follow Wangongi's son Jesus. Following Jesus leads us to a great village, a village we call heaven. But, if we do not follow Wangongi's carvings, we follow a trail to a dark jungle where Wangongi does not live.

Betty Our husbands followed Wangongi's carvings. They believed in His son, Jesus. They walked His trail. We know they are in heaven with Wangongi.

Barb I wonder what the men are doing in heaven right now?

Marj I think they have been greeted – "well done, my good and faithful servants". They are in the presence of God and are surely experiencing a comfort we cannot imagine here on earth.

Betty Wouldn't it be wonderful if Christ returned right now, uniting us with the fellas and Himself in the air?

Rachel Christ will come again only when every tribe, every tongue has heard the gospel. Until then, we must continue in our own callings.

Marj And, Marilou, for you that means preparing for the birth of this baby. Your decision is much more urgent than ours, and we're here to help with anything you and the boys need.

Marj I know, Marj. I know I have a tremendous support system here, but I think I need to return to Michigan, at least until the baby is born. I can stay with my parents, and they will help with the boys. I think it will also be a comfort to both my parents and to Ed's to have Steve and Michael close by. We've been in the jungle since Stevie was born, and the boys need to know their grandparents.

   (Olive weeps uncontrollably.)

Betty Olive, stop that! You've got to stop feeling sorry for yourself.

Olive I can't help it. I know I need to be strong right now, but my heart is in my throat. The tears dam up behind my eyes until I just cannot physically hold them back any longer.

Betty But are you're crying because you have lost Pete or because you're not trusting God to see you through this?

Olive I don't know, I really don't. Perhaps it is a lack of faith. Pete was always so sure of what God wanted from him. I don't know that I've ever felt that way. And, I'm sure I don't understand any of this. How could God allow Pete, let any of these men be taken like this?

Betty God promises us He will not give us more than we can bear.

Olive I know the scriptures. And I do get a sense of peace when reading God's promises, I do. But, then this wave of grief comes over me, and I just have to ask – I'm 21 years old, my husband, my hope for children, it's all gone. How much does God think I can bear? And, for what? For 50 Indians? Fifty Indians who have probably retreated deep into the jungle by now and still don't know God.

Barb Olive, listen to me. Roger and I both struggled with some of the same questions you are asking yourself now. We gave all we had to the Ashuaras and saw nothing in return. The tribe's refusal to accept God spun us into a depression that nearly sent us back to the States. Now, I'm not going to claim to have the answers to all your questions, but I know this – God is sovereign. Even when we don't understand the circumstances he has placed us in, His promises are true. His Word will not come back void.

Marj Barb's right. God is moving, and we are only seeing part of the story right now. Maybe it was all for just 50 Indians, and maybe it was for some other purpose entirely.

Rachel Exactly. We have to trust that God is still in this. The chapter may have been written for the fellas, but God is not finished with the story. The one thing I do know is that we must stand firm in our faith, now maybe more than ever.

   (Music begins.)

SOMEBODY SAY GLORY – Martha Ford Fry

Marj We're all hurting right now. I've been up all night myself, asking the Lord "What now?" But the Lord knows our hurts, and He's the only one who can guide us through this.

Song Suggestions:

Who Am I? Words and Music by John Mark Hall (Performance Rights Required)

Take My Life and Let It Be. Words by Frances Ridley Havergal and Music by Louis Joseph Ferdinand Herold (Public Domain)

He Leadeth Me. Words by Joseph Henry Gilmore and Music by William Batchelder Bradbury (Public Domain)

(Music continues to play behind the dialogue.)

Betty I am God's. I was called to be a missionary before I married Jim, and I know that this is His will for my life. Valerie and I will stay here and continue to work with the Quechuas.

Rachel As soon as we help Marilou pack up Arajuno, Dayuma and I will return to Hacienda Ila. But, we'll be here any time any of you need us.

Marilou While I'm returning to the States for now, I know my work isn't finished here. The boys and I will be back as soon as I'm able.

Barb Roger worked too hard to reach the Ashuara people for me to give up on them now. We were so close to leaving at one point, but God clearly directed our paths to stay here. He would want me to continue what we started. Jerry and Beth and I will remain here.

Marj Shell Mera is a home for a missionary pilot. I don't think I should stay here. Abe Van Der Puy has been looking for someone to run the HCJB guesthouse for the past two years. I think that would be a good position for me, and I could still care for the children.

Olive Pete and I never talked about what I would do if he died. I never finished my college studies, and I'm not really trained in anything except missionary medicine. I'm going to go back to Seattle and pray about what God would have me do next. My future is in His hands.

MUSIC AND LIGHTS FADE OUT

SOMEBODY SAY GLORY – Martha Ford Fry

ACT II

SCENE 2

A WOMAN'S TOUCH

Scene:

Jungle in Ecuador, clearing at center stage.

>(Rachel *and* Dayuma *sit at a table working on language translation. Enter* Betty, Mintaka *and* Gimari.*)*

Betty *(Breathless)* Rachel, Dayuma. You're not going to believe this. The Quechua came out to me at Shandia. Two Auca women had left the jungle and wandered into the village. I couldn't believe it, but, when I got there, sure enough there stood two Auca women.

>(Betty *stands aside, revealing and pointing to* Mintaka *and* Gimari *standing behind her.* Dayuma *rises and hugs* Mintaka *and* Gimari.*)*

Dayuma Gimari, Mintaka.

Mintaka Dayuma? Is it really you?

Dayuma Yes, it is me. I did not think I would ever see my family again.

Gimari Oh, Dayuma. We thought the foreigners had eaten you.

>(Mintaka *and* Gimari *spin* Dayuma *around, examining her body.)*

Mintaka You have not been speared by the foreigners?

Dayuma No, these foreigners are good. They do not spear.

Rachel Dayuma, you know these women?

Dayuma *(To* Rachel *and* Betty*)* Yes, they are my family. This is Gimari – she is my little sister. And, this,

>*(Pointing to* Mintaka.*)*

Dayma *(Continues)* This is my aunt, Mintaka.

Rachel Ask them why they have left the jungle.

Dayuma *(To* Mintaka *and* Gimari*)* What brings you to the Quechua village?

Mintaka I am old, Dayuma, and I am tired of the killing.

Gimari But we need help if we are going to stop the spearing.

Dayuma Tell me. Tell me of my family. My mother, Akawo, does she still live?

Mintaka Your mother lives. She has cried out for you all the days you have been gone.

Dayuma And my sister, Oba, and my brothers, Nampa and Wawae, do they still live?

Gimari Our brothers are dead. Both Nampa and Wawae.

    *(*Dayuma *puts her hands to her face, staving off tears.)*

Dayuma How, how? Being speared, were they buried and then died?

Gimari Nampa was not speared.

Mintaka He was crushed by a giant boa while hunting in the jungle.

Gimari He lived until the next full moon.

Mintaka The downriver people cursed his soul. He died a slow, painful death.

Dayuma And, Wawae…

Gimari Wawae was speared when Moipa tried to take our village.

Mintaka Please, Dayuma, you must come back to the tribe.

Gimari Teach us the way of these foreigners.

Mintaka Teach us to live without spearing.

Gimari At the next full moon we return to the village.

Mintaka Go with us, Dayuma.

Rachel Betty, why don't you take these women to get something to eat? I need to talk to Dayuma.

    (Exit Betty, Mintaka, *and* Gimari.*)*

Dayuma They want me to return to the jungle with them. They are tired of the killing and want me to teach them your ways.

Rachel I think you should go with them, Dayuma.

Dayuma But…

SOMEBODY SAY GLORY – Martha Ford Fry

(Pause.)

Rachel But, what?

Dayuma I still fear my mother. She promised to kill me when my father was speared.

Rachel That was a long time ago. These women, your family, are tired of the killing. Your mother surely is tired of the killing as well.

Dayuma And, what if I do return? What if my mother is happy to see me? The men are still killing. They have killed my brother Wawae. They killed your brother, Nate, and his friends. What if those men are not tired of the killing?

Rachel Dayuma, do you remember when we were in New York City and you met Dr. Billy Graham?

Dayuma Of course, yes.

Rachel Well, Dr. Graham once questioned Wangongi and His truth.

Dayuma Dr. Graham questioned Wangoni? But he tells many people they must believe Wangongi's carvings, they must follow His trail.

Rachel Yes, now he tells people they must follow Wangoni's Son, Jesus Christ. But one day, he questioned the truth in Wangongi's Carvings. On that day, he took His Bible and went out into a forest near his home – a jungle of trees just like here – to talk to Wangongi. And, after he had talked to Wangongi for a long time, he made a decision.

(Rachel takes her Bible, opens it, and places it on a tree stump.)

Rachel *(Continued)* He took his Bible, Wangongi's Carvings, and placed them open on a tree stump just like this. Dr. Graham told Wangongi - that day, in that jungle - that he was going to believe everything that was in those Carvings, and he promised Wangongi that he would follow His trail all the days of his life.

(Pause.)

Rachel *(Continues)* Dayuma, I believe today is the day you must make the same decision.

(Pause.)

Rachel *(Continues)* You may be speared if you return to the village – just like my brother Nate and his friends were speared when they tried to take Wangongi's Carvings to your people. But, Dayuma, you may be the only person who can tell your people about Wangongi and His great love for them without being speared.

(Rachel places her hand on the open Bible and gently pats it.)

SOMEBODY SAY GLORY - Martha Ford Fry

Rachel *(Continues)* But, just as Dr. Graham could not tell those people in New York to follow Wangongi if he did not believe it, you, Dayuma, cannot tell the Auca if you don't believe it.

    (Rachel moves to exit stage right. She stops halfway and turns back to Dayuma. Music begins.)

Rachel And, Dayuma, you must believe that Wangongi…

    (Rachel points into the jungle behind Dayuma at stage left.)

Rachel *(Continues)* is already there.

    (Exit Rachel. Dayuma kneels in prayer over the Bible. She looks up, still kneeling.)

Song Suggestions:

I Know You're There. Words and Music by Jeff Chandler (Performance Rights Required)

Anywhere With Jesus. Words by Jessie Brown Pounds; verse 3 by Mrs. C.M.A.; Music by D. B. Towner (Public Domain)

    (Music continues, Dayuma picks up the Bible, closes it and places it under her arm.)

Dayuma *(Determinedly)* Following Him, I will go.

    (Exit Dayuma.)

                                        MUSIC AND LIGHTS FADE OUT

ACT II

SCENE THREE

SALVATION

Scene:

Jungle in Ecuador.

> *(Enter* Dayuma, *walking across stage to table and benches, drying her hair. Sounds of leaves rustling and twigs breaking in the background.* Dayuma *cocks her head to listen.)*

Dayuma Is someone there?

> *(Pause. Leaves rustle again.)*

Dayuma Is someone out there?

> *(*Kimo *emerges from the jungle darkness.)*

Dayuma Kimo. What brings you here tonight?

> *(Pause.)*

Dayuma *(Continues)* Do you need something?

> *(Pause.)*

Dayuma *(Continues)* Are you hurt?

> *(Pause.)*

Kimo *(Hesitantly)* I've been thinking, Dayuma.

> *(Pause.)*

Dayuma *(Gingerly)* About what, Kimo?

Kimo About what you have been teaching us about Wangongi.

> *(Pause.)*

Dayuma Yes, Kimo? What about Wangongi troubles you?

Kimo I know you have told us that Wangongi loves us. Loves us so much, He sent His only Son to be speared for us. But, Dayuma,

> *(Pause.)*

Kimo *(Continues)* Dayuma. What about one with a heart as black as mine? Can Wangongi love one with such a black heart?

Dayuma Oh, yes, Kimo. Wangongi loves you as much as He loves me, and the blood of His Son can cleanse the blackest of hearts.

Kimo What must I do for Wangongi to cleanse my black heart?

Dayuma Kimo, you must admit that your heart is black and that you cannot cleanse it yourself. You must believe that Wangongi's Son, Jesus Christ, was speared and shed His blood so that Wangongi could forgive you and cleanse your black heart.

> *(Dayuma takes a Bible from the table, opens it, and points to a verse.)*

Dayuma *(Continues)* Right here in Wangongi's carvings, Kimo, He tells us "anyone who is in Christ Jesus becomes a new creature. The old things are passed away, and all things become new." This can be you, Kimo. Wangongi can make your old black heart, into a new one. You just have to ask Him.

Kimo I have lived this way a long time. I have speared, speared many people. I just do not know if Wangongi could really love one such as me.

Dayuma He can, Kimo. He promises that if you follow His trail, He will remove your old life, the spearing, from your path. Just ask Him, and you will see. He will release you from the chains of spearing.

> *(Music begins. Exit Dayuma. Lights dim. Spotlight up on Kimo.)*

Song Suggestions:

Set Me Free. Words and Music by John Mark Hall and Bernie Herms (Performance Rights Required)

Chief of Sinners. Words by McComb; Music; Spanish Tune (Public Domain)

Shall I Be Saved Tonight. Words by Frances Jane Crosby and Music By Mrs. N. Bliss Wilson (Public Domain)

SPOTLIGHT OFF

SOMEBODY SAY GLORY - Martha Ford Fry

ACT II

SCENE FOUR

GOD FOLLOWERS

Scene:

Jungle in Ecuador.

> *(*Gikita *and* Mincaye *braid vines. Enter* Dayuma. *Music begins as* Dayuma *sits and pulls the stems from berries. As* Dayuma *begins to sing,* Gikita *and* Mincaye *stop work momentarily and then go back to their tasks.)*

Director's Note: This song can be cut for time. Or, only the chorus can be sung as a brief introduction showing the characters worshipping and praising while doing ordinary tasks.

Song Suggestions:

Praise You with the Dance. Words and Music by John Mark Hall (Performance Rights Required)

Blessed Be The Name. Words by William H. Clark; Music by Ralph E. Hudson (Public Domain)

> *(Enter* Kimo *in the middle of the song.* Kimo *joins* Dayuma, *sharpening his spear as he sings.* Gikita *and* Mincaye *stop working and watch in disbelief. When the song is finished* Kimo *and* Dayuma *continue working and* Gikita *and* Mincaye *approach them.)*

Mincaye Kimo, have you been drinking bad manioc?

Gikita You are acting like one with bad spirits.

Kimo No, no Mincaye, no bad manioc. And, no, Gikita, no bad spirits. No, a good spirit.

Mincaye What are you talking about? What good spirit has possessed you and made you to act like this?

Kimo The only Good Spirit. The Spirit of Wangongi.

Gikita *(Examining* Kimo *for spear marks)* He must have been speared and has lost much blood. He talks nonsense.

SOMEBODY SAY GLORY - Martha Ford Fry

Kimo I have not been speared, but Wangongi's son, Jesus, was speared and He has bled. His strong blood has washed my black heart, a heart that was dark like night is now cleansed, and that is why I can sing – and dance.

Gikita You have listened to the foreigners – and to Dayuma.

Mincaye The foreigners turned her into a silly girl, but you, Kimo, we thought you smarter than that.

Kimo I am smart – smart to listen when Wangongi speaks.

Gikita What are you talking about?

Kimo Nimu and Dayuma have Wangongi's Carvings.

    (Kimo *pulls a small book out of* Dayuma*'s basket. Music begins.*)

Kimo Wangongi tells us in His Carvings that He does not wish that we spear or be speared. That is why He sent His Son, Jesus, to be speared once for all of us. This is what the foreigners we killed came to tell us. That is why they did not use guns against us.

Mincaye Gikita, Kimo speaks truth in that. We know the foreigners had guns.

Kimo Yes, they could have killed us. They could have fled into the jungle and hid from us. But they wanted us to know this Jesus. Just like we speared the good foreigners, so people speared God's good son, Jesus. He was speared so we could live with Wangongi. See it is here, here in His Carvings.

    (Kimo *opens the Bible and shows* Mincaye *and* Gikita *the text.*)

Song Suggestions:

My Lifesong Sings. Words and Music by John Mark Hall (Performance Rights Required)

Blessed Assurance. Words by Frances Jane Crosby; Music by Phoebe Palmer Knapp (Public Domain)

Mincaye Before, not understanding, I killed, but now Jesus' blood washes my heart clean – I will no longer hate, but will live with a heart that is healed.

    *(*Gikita *stands.)*

Gikita One day, we shall see those good foreigners again in the village you are preparing for us, and seeing them and your son Jesus, who was speared for us, we will be happy.

    (All kneel together in prayer.)

                                                  FADE OUT

ACT II

SCENE FIVE

TROUBLE

Scene

Jungle in Ecuador.

> (Kimo *and* Mincaye *sit on stumps around a fire arguing. Spears are propped around them.*)

Mincaye We must avenge these killings.

Kimo That is not what Wangongi God would want us to do.

Mincaye If the downriver tribe finds us weak, we will be slaughtered.

Kimo We need to speak to Nimu and Dayuma. They know what to do.

Mincaye We will be speared. Our wives will be taken as slaves. This is the Waodani way. Nimu knows nothing of this way of life, and Dayuma no longer remembers.

Kimo But Dayuma knows Wangongi's ways. She knows much more of His Carvings than we do.

> (Enter Dayuma *and* Rachel, *stopping before they reach the men, listening.*)

Mincaye She barely remembers her own language, let alone the ways of her people.

> (Mincaye *stands.*)

Mincaye *(Continues)* I tell you - We must spear or be speared.

> (Dayuma *and* Rachel *come up to the men.* Mincaye *sits back down as he sees her, avoiding eye contact with the women.*)

Dayuma I may not remember all things Waodani, but I do remember how we lived. Spearing was never the answer. What is it you are planning, Mincaye?

Mincaye We must retaliate against the attack on our village.

Rachel No, Mincaye. You know Wangongi has said in His Carvings, 'You must not kill.'

Dayuma Fear now returns to our village. If we are weak, we are vulnerable. Our enemies will attack, and they will spear again.

Rachel And, Kimo, what say you?

Kimo I have placed my trust in Wangongi, and I know His word is true. But,

Dayuma *(Angrily)* But, what?

Kimo But I also know the ways of this jungle. And, in that, Mincaye is right. The spears will come. And when they do, will Wangongi stop them?

Dayuma Have you asked Wangongi to stop them?

Mincaye No.

Rachel Mincaye, Wangongi God has taken your past sins and thrown them as far as the east is from the west. You cannot return to the man you used to be.

    (Music begins.)

Kimo Dayuma is right. Before we do this thing, we go to Wangongi God.

    (All kneel in prayer. Kimo rises.)

Song Suggestions:

East to West. Words and Music by Bernie Herms and John Mark Hall. (Performance Rights Required)

Trust and Obey. Words by John H. Sammis and Music by Daniel Brink Towner (Pubic Domain)

Come Closer to Me. Words and Music by Barney E. Warren. (Public Domain)

    (Music ends. Enter Gimari. Mincaye, Dayuma, Rachel, *and* Kimo *lower their arms and turn towards her.)*

Gimari *(Breathless)* Mincaye, Dayuma come!

    (Gimari takes Mincaye *and* Dayuma *by their arms and pulls them as if she wants them to go with her. Dayuma wrestles loose from her grasp.)*

Dayuma Slow down, girl. What is wrong?

Gimari You must come back to the village. It is Toné.

    (Gimari lets go of Mincaye*'s arm and bends over to catch her breath.)*

SOMEBODY SAY GLORY – Martha Ford Fry

Kimo Toné? The one who speared our family? Has he speared again?

    (Gimari shakes her head in the negative.)

Gimari No, he is dead.

Rachel Oh, no. Has someone speared him?

Gimari No, Nimu. No one speared.

Mincaye If no one speared, how is he dead?

Gimari He is just dead. In the middle of the village he fell - dead. Just as if Wangongi struck him dead.

    *(*Mincaye, Kimo, Rachel, *and* Dayuma *look at each other in fearful astonishment.)*

                                              FADE OUT

SOMEBODY SAY GLORY - Martha Ford Fry

ACT II

SCENE SIX

RECONCILIATION

Scene:

Former Saint home, Shell Mera, Ecuador, June 13, 1992.

>*(Kimo, Gikita, Mincaye, Steve Saint, and Matt McCully are in the kitchen. Stacks of Wao Bibles sit on the table.)*

Matt McCully It seems strange to be here, here in this place that changed my dad's life – a dad I never even got to meet.

Steve Saint I've been here many times, and it's always the same – bittersweet. This is where our fathers planned Operation Auca. Over there in the shed

>*(Steve Saint points out through the kitchen window.)*

Steve Saint *(Continues)* that's where the little yellow model planes were built.

>*(Steve Saint points a little farther over.)*

Steve Saint *(Continues)* And on that runway, the yellow Piper flew out for the last time. But I know in my heart that our fathers died the way they would have wanted to die – doing the will of God.

Kimo Your fathers never got to see the fruits of their labors, but they planted the seed.

Gikita Nimu and Gikari watered the ground

Mincaye As they taught us

Kimo Another way to live,

Gikita Not by the spear,

Kimo But by the carvings

Mincaye Of Creator God.

Gikita And, now you continue the task…

>*(Kimo touches the stacks of Bibles on the table.)*

Kimo bringing us more of Wangongi God's Carvings.

(Kimo picks up one of the Bibles from the table and raises it in his hand. Looking upward.)

Kimo Father God, You who are alive, all powerful, all knowing. We have come here to worship You.

(Gikita places his hand on the stack of Bibles on the table.)

Gikita Today we have Your Carvings, enough for all Waodani.

Mincaye We receive it happily. Before we were empty-handed, but,

(Mincaye picks up a Bible.)

Mincaye *(Continues)* Having received it, we accept it saying, 'This is truth.'

Gikita Father God, listen! We say to you 'We obey Your Carving.' Following Your trail, we live well. Yes, as long as we are on this earth, forever and ever.

Matt McCully Amen.

All Amen.

(As Gikita, Mincaye, and Kimo stand still in prayer. Matt McCully and Steve Saint come to the front of the stage.)

Matt McCully People often hear the story of our fathers and think of the sadness of five young men being speared to death.

Steve Saint But, our fathers did not have their lives taken by the Auca. Our fathers, and our mothers, had long ago given their lives – given them to the Lord.

(Music begins.)

Matt McCully Theirs is but a chapter in the story of how God is fulfilling His promise that some from every tribe, every nation will come to worship the Lord as God. And, now we stand here, speaking different tongues, but sharing one voice as we worship Wangongi God, His Spirit that guides our walk, and His Son, Jesus Christ, who was speared so that we could live with Him forever.

Steve Saint Somebody say Glory!

Song Suggestions:

Father, Spirit, Jesus. Words and Music by Chad Cates, John Mark Hall, David Hunt (Performance Rights Required)

Since Jesus Came Into My Heart. Words by Rufus Henry McDaniel and Music by Charles Hutchinson Gabriel (Public Domain)

                                                FADE OUT

                                THE END

SOMEBODY SAY GLORY - Martha Ford Fry

SOMEBODY SAY GLORY - Martha Ford Fry

BONUS SCENE

THE LAST CHRISTMAS

Director's Note:

This scene was originally staged in Act I as Scene Six. As originally written and performed with all music, the play may run longer than desired for most amateur productions. As a result, this scene was cut from subsequent productions. It is provided here as a bonus scene to be used at the discretion of producers.

Scene:

Saint home in Shell Mera, Ecuador.

> *(*Marj *reads Christmas cards at the kitchen table. Enter* Nate, *carrying a box of Christmas ornaments into the living room, where other boxes sit partially unpacked in front of a naked Christmas tree. A nativity set on the mantel. As* Nate *crosses into the living room,* Marj *looks up from the cards.)*

Marj Nate, there were Christmas cards from our folks in the mailbag you picked up in Quito today.

Nate What's the news from back home?

Marj Everyone's excited about Christmas. Sam will be coming home, so I guess our family and Rachel will be the only ones missing at your folks this year. They've sent presents for the children and hope we receive them before Christmas morning.

Nate *(Sarcastically)* Oh, yes, that would be quite the tragedy if the children failed to receive their presents in time for Christmas morning.

Marj Nate Saint. That doesn't sound like you. You love Christmas, and I never see a bigger smile on your face then when the children are opening their presents.

Nate I guess I just feel differently about it this year.

Marj And why is that, dear? I would think with Operation Auca going so well this would be the most joyous Christmas season ever.

Nate *(Holding up a Christmas ornament)* The holidays just don't hold the same joy as in years past, maybe because of the success of Operation Auca.

Marj How so, dear?

SOMEBODY SAY GLORY – Martha Ford Fry

Nate We've grown to accept the Christmas season as a time of joyfulness, celebration – full of twinkling lights and the sounds of carolers. Even here, in the darkness of this jungle, we are pulling out glass balls and tinsel. Yet, we sit literally at the doorstep of an entire people group who have no Christmas. And this is not a tragedy because they have no stockings to hang or presents to unwrap, but because they have no Christ. I want so desperately to be celebrating Christmas with the Aucas.

Marj Nate, I know that this need for secrecy and your inability to ask for specific prayer has been troubling you.

Nate We've never not been able to share our prayer needs before. And, we need the prayers of Christians right now more than the children need presents from the States.

Marj But, these cards and letters are evidence that our friends and family are sacrificially supporting us, not only financially, but through prayer.

Nate *(Impatiently, almost angrily)* But, isn't that just a bit ironic? - That Christians should even consider it a "sacrifice" to forego a little merriment and merchandise in order to take the time to pray and give some money for God's work?

*(*Nate *motions to the nativity set on the mantel.)*

Nate Have we learned nothing from the people of Bethlehem? On that first Christmas night, as the Savior of the world was being born in a dark and dingy stable, the people of Bethlehem slept, just as the Aucas sleep this night in the darkness of the jungle – completely unaware of this great gift that God has given us. But worse yet, how many of us, how many who have had the privilege of knowing the true meaning of Christmas, how many of us will be found to be sleeping when Christ comes again?

Baby *(Cries offstage.)*

*(*Marj *glances at the door to the radio room and back at* Nate*.)*

Nate Go on and tend to Phillip. I'm just going to pick up a few things here and get the lights. I'll be along shortly.

*(*Marj *walks over and kisses* Nate*.)*

Marj Don't stay up too late.

(Exit Marj *through the radio room door off the kitchen. Music begins.* Nate *pulls another piece of the nativity scene from the box and walks over to the mantel and places it on the mantel, then plugs in a star hanging above the mantel.)*

Song Suggestions:

While You Were Sleeping Words and Music by Mark Hall. (Performance Rights Required)

    Director's Note: The second verse of this song can be cut for time purposes.

Hasten Today. Words and Music by Daniel O. Teasley (Public Domain)

(Nate moves over to the kitchen table and picks up a few of the Christmas cards scattered there, looking at them as if to read one. Nate lays the Christmas cards down on the table, moves over to doorway to the radio room. Flipping off the light, Exit Nate.)

                                            FADE OUT

(Stage is dark as the last lines of the song are heard. If the hymn is used, Nate should sing "Silent Night, Holy Night" from offstage.)

Performance Rights

Public Performances

Protection against unlawful performances of plays is provided by United States Copyright Law. No public performance or reading of a protected play may be given, either in its entirety or in the form of excerpts, without the prior consent of the Copyright Owner. Austin House Publishing, as agent for the author and copyright owner Martha Ford Fry, issues licenses for the performance of the Play Script "Somebody Say Glory." If copyrighted songs are used, Performance Rights are required to be obtained from the copyright owner of each song. Songs used which are in the Public Domain at the time of performance are not subject to Performance Rights.

Performance Rights

All requests for Performance Rights should be mailed to:

Martha Ford Fry
Austin House Publishing
318 Dylan Way
McDonough, GA 30252

All requests should include the following information:

Contact Name
Group or Organization
Address
Contact Phone Number
Contact Email
Performance Date
Number of Performances
Seating Capacity of Venue
Ticketed or Free Event
Amateur or Professional Performance

Photocopying Rights

Photocopying Rights may be requested with Performance Rights. If you would prefer to purchase Play Script books, a discounted bulk rate can be obtained by contacting Austin House Publishing.

Publicity

All notices, posters, flyers, programs, advertisements, radio and TV broadcasts must acknowledge the author of the Play Script as Martha Ford Fry.

Prior Consent

It is important that Performance Rights be obtained before any performance of a play is given. Austin House Publishing only provides Performance Rights for the Play Script. If Performance Rights are requested after the event, a Penalty Payment, in addition to the appropriate Performance Rights fee, may apply for each performance given.

Video Recordings

It should not be assumed that any play may be video recorded for any purpose without first obtaining the permission of the appropriate agents. Video rights must be obtained from Austin House Publishing for the Play Script. If copyrighted songs are used in the performance, Video Rights must be obtained from the copyright holders of each song. Austin House Publishing holds no rights to any of the songs suggested for use with the Play Script.

www.ingramcontent.com/pod-product-compliance
Lightning Source LLC
Chambersburg PA
CBHW081219230426
43666CB00015B/2808